a gift for:

from:

Copyright © 2010 Hallmark Licensing, Inc.

Published by Hallmark Books,
a division of Hallmark Cards, Inc.,
Kansas City, MO 64141
Visit us on the Web at www.Hallmark.com.

Art Director: Kevin Swanson
Designer: Mary Eakin
Production Designer: Bryan Ring

ISBN: 978-1-59530-324-0
BOK3103
Printed and bound in China
JUL10

Hallmark
GIFT BOOKS

When You Need to Know Your Strength

messages of hope and healing

for women living with cancer

By Melvina Young

CONTENTS

for you . . .

Receiving a diagnosis of cancer has to be one of the hardest and scariest things anybody can go through. It's one of those times in life that can leave even the strongest person staggering and in need of loved ones to lean on.

When a beloved relative and a couple of dear friends of mine were diagnosed, I wanted desperately to offer words of encouragement and hope. I wanted to express my love and support. Instead, I found myself at a loss for what to say.

They were scared and I was scared for them. Plus, as absurd as it seems given the circumstances, I was worried that I might say the wrong thing...and sometimes I did. Still, the message I got back from my loved ones was, "I'd rather have you say something and risk saying it badly, than say nothing like this wasn't happening to me."

I started wondering what someone who's heard "It's cancer" needed family and friends to say. I started listening more closely to those people. They said things like "I don't know why this is happening. I'm scared. I'm angry. I'm tired. I'm sick, but I don't need pity. I'm still the same person, and I need the same love from the people around me."

This book is, in part, a result of that listening and learning. I tried to recognize many of the widely ranging feelings fighting cancer can bring up. One moment a person might feel like a warrior, ready to face the battle head-on, but in the next wanting retire to a private island on the outer banks of imagination. Sometimes that same person might be overjoyed by all the love shown by supporters, but in the next be unaccountably angry with everybody and everything.

The battle against cancer is a very personal experience, different for every man or woman. So, the various pieces of writing included here are meant to acknowledge each reader for who they are and what they may be feeling in the moment. They are here for when someone might need to feel encouraged, strengthened, loved or emotionally affirmed.

I hope that this book helps you support a loved one with cancer. Maybe that loved one is you.

for when
you need
encouragement

Trouble walked in
    and got all up in your face—
demanding, loud,
        and soul-draining.

But if you can sit still for a while
  in the presence of your own spirit,
you may find hidden springs of

peace
  and strength.

Giving up control is tough.

But what if we could
        think about it as
learning to ride the current
        instead of always trying
to swim against the tide?

This has been hard on you.
So why be hard on yourself?

Treat yourself like you'd
treat a best friend.

Nurture yourself

like you would anybody else

going through something this hard.

Forgive yourself

for not being perfect.

Who is?

Mere humans have
wrestled with giants . . .
and won.

Just something to consider.

Even on dark days,
we can look to the
light spaces in the clouds
and know that
the sun is
still there.

Why should you
stop the tears
when they want to come?

Sorrow is looking
for a way out.
So are fear and anger.
Why not show them
the exit?

Then maybe things

you need more, like

laughter,

hope,

and strength,

can move in and live

in sorrow's old room.

We like to think that we master our own lives,
that being a good person
and playing by the rules
will bring good things.

That's one of the little promises
we subconsciously make to ourselves
before getting out of bed each day.

Cancer doesn't care about that.
It doesn't care about rules or promises.

That's why we can't care what cancer thinks.
We have to listen hardest to faith.
Believe most strongly in hope.

Lean on faith.
Let hope **hold your hand**.

Change happens from moment to moment –

hold out hope that
some of it will be good.

You're the sum of all the things
that came before this
and all the things
that will come after.

You're more than
what is happening to you
right now.

You **always** were
and you **always** will be.

When the angel on your right shoulder says,

"Stay strong!"

and the one on your left says,

"Chocolate and a movie,"

sometimes it's good to listen

to the one on the left.

Along your
path of healing,
may there be
forest beds of wisdom,
growing gardens of compassion,

and flowing rivers of hope.

It's hard to believe right now,
but the day is coming
when your first thought
when you wake up
or your last thought
when you close your eyes at night
won't be "cancer."

When you can go back to thinking about
some wonderfully mundane thing like
good coffee or bad traffic or
hot office romances or awful reality shows or
"do these jeans make my butt look big?"

When you can look back
on this chapter in your life
and turn the page for what's coming next.

That will be a wonderful day.

In the book of all the world's great events . . .

there is you beating this.

for when you need
to know

your strength

Breaking down.

Cracking up.

Coming apart.

It's just a natural part
of what you sometimes have to do
to hold yourself together.

Usually when
someone fights this hard,
we give them a medal
or a trophy
or a diamond-encrusted belt.

You might not feel
like **a world-class fighter**.
But you are.

And you deserve so much more
than a medal.

If mountains were smooth . . .

how could we climb?

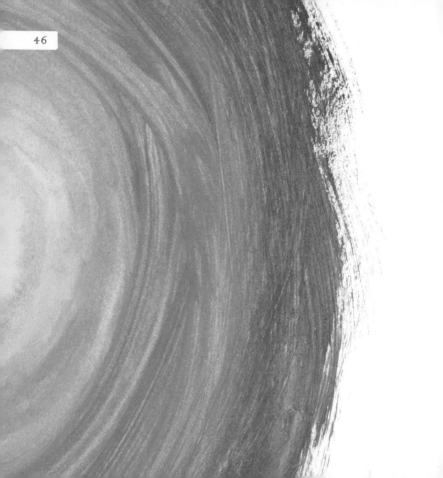

The fear may keep revealing itself layer by layer.

But so will **your strength**.

The thing about strength
is that when you're
running a little low,

you can tap a friend for a refill.

The same strength
that got you this far
is still **inside you** . . .

waiting to take you

wherever you need to go.

for when

it gets hard

Making peace within yourself
can be hard when you're angry
        with your own body.

How could it take cancer's side over your's?

It gets hard
with everybody calling you brave
when you've never been so scared
in your life.

This is not your body's fault.

It's cancer,
intruder and blowhard bully,
who just moved on in
and set up camp
despite anything your body
has to say about it.

Your body's an innocent bystander.
So are you.

Even the people who love you most
        may say or do the wrong thing
    when trying to show how much they care.

But this is only temporary.

Love is for always.

Tears don't measure weakness.
They measure your strength to grieve
and **keep on going**.

It can seem like
the finish line
keeps moving ten feet ahead
of where you just crossed.

And even though
you've got no choice
but to tighten your laces
and try again,
you are admired for it.

Wiping down fears,
sweeping up worries,
and dusting off dreams
can take up all your energy.

It's your emotional house.

Put it in any order you want.

Sometimes

"weathering the storm"

means closing all the windows and
putting up the shutters.

Other times it means sitting in the rain
and letting the raindrops tap out
a soft rhythm on your sky-turned face.

But when the spirit moves -

it means

out-shouting the thunder

and out-crying the rain.

Whichever **feels right** is right.

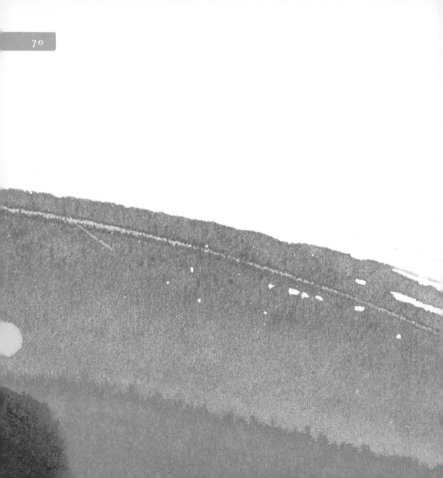

Sometimes when life sets you down

at the crossroads,

it's time to draw a new map.

Sometimes there is no reason.

Unless "**unfair**" is a reason.

When anybody
for any reason
asks you to
"put on a **happy face**,"
feel free to keep wearing
your **real** one.

They'll just have to deal with it.

Cancer will turn your "cusser" on.

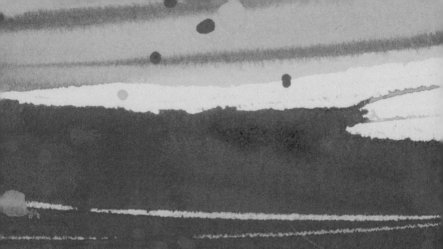

Well @#$% Cancer!

Cancer sucks.

It sucks up your energy.
It sucks up your time.
It sucks out your bank account.
It will even try to suck
all the color from your world.

Cancer just plain sucks.

If it's supposed to make you better,

why does it have wear you out?

Sometimes you've just got to lie down.

Rest your body.

Release your mind.

Nurture your spirit.

Get **your strength** back.

Try again.

for when

you need to know

you are loved

Standing at this threshold is scary,

because you don't know

what's beyond the door.

But the people who love you

are ready to **take your hand**

and walk through with you.

Whenever you are ready.

Strength,

like a river,

might ebb and flow.

Faith,

like a bird,

might take flight.

Love,

like a mountain,

is always sturdy and

always, always there.

When the sky falls,
it's the ones who love you
who will help you pick it up

and rehang it,

piece by piece.

It's only a burden

when you don't share it

with the ones who love you.

When you feel like
you're losing your grip . . .

remember:
the people who love you
will be right there,
putting their shoulders
against the load
to help you shore it up.

Have you counted lately
the number of people
who are on your side?

Get comfortable.

That may take you a while.

On this journey

it's okay to **stop**,

rest, and **lean**

on fellow travelers

for a while.

Then, when you have

your strength back,

you can move on,

surrounded in love
by the people who care for you.

The ones who
will **walk with you**
every step of the way.

Until life starts treating you more gently,

people who care about you will.

Waiting rooms, **waiting** for tests,
waiting for results.

Until life gets easier, let those who love you **wait with you**. Or for you. Or on you.

When counting your blessings,
start with you.

Other people do.

There's a difference between
pity and compassion.

Pity feels sorry for you.
Compassion loves you.

You are wrapped in **compassion**.

When it feels like
the whirlwind might
blow you away,
think of how **deeply rooted**
you are by love,

how held down you are

by the people who care about you.

A reassuring whisper to the battered soul,
a calming song to the shaken spirit . . .

this is the way love works.

Even though things have changed,
it's important to keep knowing
what you've always known . . .

you are loved.

If this book has touched your life

or has touched someone you know,

we would love to hear from you.

Please write to us:
Hallmark Book Feedback
P.O. Box 419034
Mail Drop 215
Kansas City, MO 64141

Or e-mail:
booknotes@hallmark.com